T0132464

Some of God's Creatures

Barbara K. Floyd

Copyright © 2023 by Barbara K. Floyd. 852353

All rights reserved. No part of this book may
be reproduced or transmitted in any form or by
any means, electronic or mechanical, including
photocopying, recording, or by any information
storage and retrieval system, without permission
in writing from the copyright owner.

Illustrated by Salvador Capuyan.

To order additional copies of this book, contact:
Xlibris
844-714-8691
www.Xlibris.com
Orders@Xlibris.com

ISBN: Softcover   979-8-3694-0213-9
       Hardcover   979-8-3694-0214-6
       EBook   979-8-3694-0212-2

Print information available on the last page

Rev. date: 08/30/2023

Some of God's Creatures

Illustrated by Salvador Capuyan

I don't know, but I've heard say

That every little dog will have his day.

That's just fine if you are a dog.

But what about a cat, hamster, bird, fish or frog?

Why is a dog said to be man's best friend?

What about a horse, lamb, goat or hen?

All animals are important in God's eyes.

That's why He made them, I'd surmise.

Horses play an important part

in this country of ours.

That was the way people traveled

before there were cars.

Horses help round up cattle that have strayed.

They sleep in the barn where they eat hay.

Some can be trained to be show horses,

prancing all regal and proud.

Some are race horses or bucking horses

at the rodeo, pleasing the crowd.

11

Lambs grow up to be sheep

and their wool is shorn,

To be used for clothing and

blankets to keep us warm.

13

In the meantime, they romp and

play in pastures green.

They're not so baaad, if you

know what I mean!

Goats are great for keeping weeds down,

Whether in the country or in town.

Soft angora wool comes from some goats,

For making soft blankets and coats.

Goat milk is also good to drink.

Try it sometime and see what you think.

A hen is a mother chicken that lays eggs.

Eggs taste so good for breakfast that Mom makes.

Most chickens are kept in a pen.

They eat worms and bugs that could

damage your garden.

A hamster is a cute little furry ball,

That likes to be held, as I recall.

He lives in a cage most of the time, or rolls

around the house in a plastic ball,

Stopping quickly when he comes to a wall.

Birds come in all sizes and beautiful colors.

That's so you can tell one kind from the other.

Some make funny noises or whistle a pretty melody.

Some can learn to talk just like you and me.

Tree frogs are little and bull frogs are big.

But they can all jump far because

they have long back legs.

Tree frogs are usually found in trees,

and bull frogs by water.

And they all make croaking sounds,

little or big, no matter.

People have races to see which frog can jump best.

The one that jumps the farthest is

crowned the winner of the contest.

Cats always seem to have a mind of their own,

Whether they are kittens or full grown.

They love to be petted and lay in your lap,

While they stretch and purr and take a nap.

They like to play with yarn or anything that moves.

And they like to hide -- sometimes in your shoe!

Fish come in all sizes and shapes.

Some live in the ocean, some in a fish tank.

Go to an aquarium and watch them swim.

Some have such vivid colors, you'll want to go again!

Each animal is special in its own way.

Yes, even dogs, can have their day!

And man's best friend could be a dog, as I recall.

But, as for me, I like them all!

How many animals can you name that
were not mentioned in this book?

1.

2.

3.

4.

5.

6.

7.

8.

9.

10.

Draw a picture of your favorite animal.

Printed in the United States
by Baker & Taylor Publisher Services